and roundnose pliers, as shown.

**2** To open the jump ring, bring one pair of pliers toward you and push the other away. Reverse the steps to close the ring.

## loops: plain

**1** Trim the wire or head pin ⅜ in. (10mm) above the top bead. Make a right-angle bend close to the bead.

**2** Grab the wire's tip with roundnose pliers. Roll the wire to form a half circle. Release the wire.

**3** Position the pliers in the loop again and continue rolling, forming a centered circle above the bead.

## loops: wrapped

**1** Make sure you have no less than 1¼ in. (32mm) of wire above your bead. With the tip of your chainnose pliers, grasp the wire directly above the bead. Bend the wire (above the pliers) into a right angle.

**2** Using roundnose pliers, position the jaws vertically in the bend.

**3** Bring the wire over the top jaw of the roundnose pliers.

**4** Keep the jaws vertical and reposition

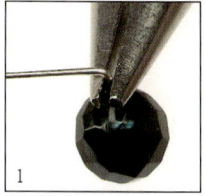

the pliers so the lower jaw fits snugly in the loop. Curve the wire downward around the bottom of the pliers.

**5** Position the jaws of your chainnose pliers across the loop.

**6** Wrap the wire around the wire stem, covering the stem between the loop and the top bead. Trim the excess wire and gently press the cut end close to the wraps with chainnose pliers.

## overhand knot

Make a loop and pass the working end through it. Pull the ends to tighten the knot.

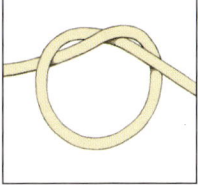

## pearl knotting

String a knotted necklace on doubled cord, starting with cord four times the desired finished length plus 8 in. (20cm). String a stop bead or bead tip and all the beads for the strand. Push everything that will follow the first knot to the needle end of the cord.

**1** Loop the cord around the first three or four fingers of your left hand (right for lefties) with the bead tip or stop bead end on top.

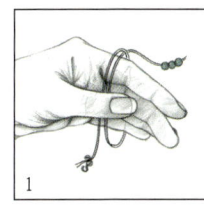

**2** Pinch the cross between your thumb and index finger. Hold the cord circle open on your fingers with your palm up. Then drop the bead end of the cord through the circle into your hand.

**3** Put a long T-pin or an awl into the loop the same way the cord goes through. Gradually tighten the loop as it slips off your fingers, keeping the awl in it. Slide the awl toward the spot where you want the knot to be

as you pull the bead end of the cord in the opposite direction. When the knot is right against the bead tip, let the cord slip off the tip of the awl. To set the knot, pull the two cord strands in opposite directions. Slide the next bead to the knot and repeat.

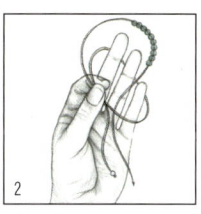
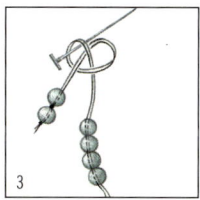

## square knot

**1** Cross the left-hand cord over the right-hand cord, and then bring it under the right-hand cord from back to front. Pull it up in front so both ends are facing upwards.

**2** Cross right over left, forming a loop, and go through the loop, again from back to front. Pull the ends to tighten the knot.

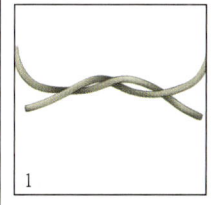
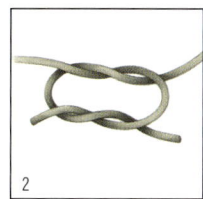

## surgeon's knot

Cross the right end over the left end and go through the loop. Go over and through again. Pull the ends to tighten.

Cross the left end over the right end and go through once. Pull the ends to tighten.

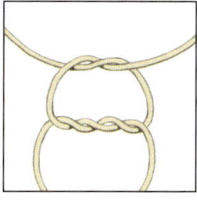

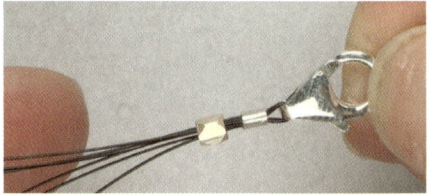
a

b

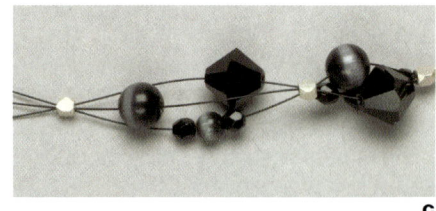
c

# Crystal clusters

Clustered together on beading wire, these groups of crystal and glass beads create a deceptively complex look. Making this necklace is easy, though, and you may find you like it so much you'll want to make a bracelet, too.

❶ Cut three 26-in. (66cm) lengths of beading wire.

❷ Pass all three wires through a crimp bead, the loop on the lobster claw, and back through the crimp bead.

❸ Crimp the crimp bead (see "Basics," p. 2).

❹ String a silver spacer over all the wires (**photo a**) and up to the crimp bead. Cut the three short wires as close to the silver spacer as possible.

❺ String an 8mm crystal on one wire and a 6mm bead on the second wire.

String a 3mm crystal, 4mm crystal, and 3mm crystal on the remaining wire. Pass all three wires through a silver spacer (**photo b**).

❻ String an 8mm crystal on one wire and a 6mm bead on the second wire, as before. String a 3mm crystal, 4mm round bead, and 3mm crystal on the remaining wire. Pass all three wires through a silver spacer (**photo c**).

❼ Repeat steps 5 and 6 until you reach the desired length.

❽ Pass all three wires through a crimp bead and a soldered jump ring. Go back through the crimp bead and the last silver spacer.

❾ Crimp the crimp bead and trim the excess wire. ● – *Anna Nehs*

## materials

- **25-28** 8mm crystal bicones
- **13-16** 4mm crystal bicones
- **50-56** 3mm fire-polished beads
- **25-28** 6mm round glass beads
- **13-16** 4mm round glass beads
- **26-29** 3mm sterling silver spacers, square or round
- **2** crimp beads
- **s**oldered jump ring
- lobster claw clasp
- flexible beading wire, size .010, colored

**Tools**: crimping pliers, wire cutter

## tip

### Plastic bags hold thread

To keep a spool of thread or beading wire from unwinding and tangling, slip it into a small zipper bag. It's easy to pull the thread out as needed and the bag never has to be opened.
– *Penny Harrell*

# Flower bracelet

Encircle your wrist in this pretty bouquet of flowers. This project can be completed quickly and it makes a great gift for yourself or someone special.

These instructions make an 8-in. (20cm) bracelet. Adjust the length for the size of your wrist by adding or omitting a flower unit. Each flower unit is approximately ½ in. (1.3cm) long.

❶ Center a seed bead on about 39 in. (1m) of Nymo. Bring the ends together and string them through a bead tip from the hook end, so the seed bead sits inside the tip (**photo a**).Close the bead tip (**photo b**).

❷ Thread both ends on a needle and, working with doubled thread, string the bracelet. *String one 6mm bead, one angel wing, one 4mm, one large flower bead, one small flower bead, and one 4mm bicone bead. Go back through the two flowers and the green 4mm bead. Add one angel wing* (**figure 1**). Repeat from * to * until your bracelet is the desired length.

❸ When you've completed the flower portion of the bracelet, add

one more 6mm bead and then string on another bead tip, this time from the end without the hook. Cut off the needle. Tighten the beads on the strand, making sure there are no gaps, but leave enough slack for the strand to drape softly. String a seed bead on one of the strands. Tie the thread ends together with a surgeon's knot (see "Basics," p. 2) over the bead (**photo c**).

❹ Glue the knot and trim the thread to about ⅛ in. (3mm) when the glue is dry. Close the second bead tip.

❺ Attach one part of the clasp to the loop of each bead tip. Use roundnose pliers to roll the hook tightly closed around the loop on the clasp. ❍

– Svitlana Nedoszytko

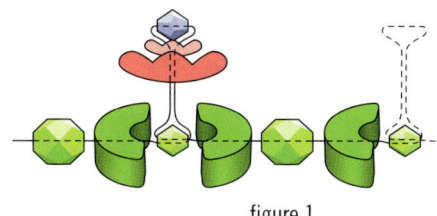

figure 1

## materials

- **18** angel wing beads, green
- **9** large flower cup beads, red
- **9** small flower cup beads, pink
- **9** 4mm faceted bicone beads, purple
- **9** 4mm fire-polished beads, green
- **10** 6mm fire-polished beads, green
- **2** size 11º seed beads
- Nymo D beading thread
- beading needle, #10
- **2** bead tips
- clasp

**Tools:** chainnose pliers and roundnose pliers

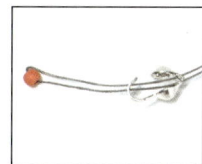

a

b

c

# Double-strand bracelet

Make an easy double-strand bracelet by using metal links that feature two holes rather than one. Combine them with other two-hole beads or your favorite stones and pearls for this elegant, sophisticated style. Complete the look with a quick pair of complementary earrings.

The pewter links shown here are made by TierraCast, which does not sell direct to consumers. Ask your local bead store, distributor, or online supplier if they carry these products. If they aren't available, you may be able to find other links or beads that will work equally well for your own design.

To determine a length that's right for you, measure your wrist and add 1 to 1½ in. (2.5-3.8cm). Changing a length is easy, but it requires planning ahead. You can add or remove a few beads at the ends or add or remove a link.

## silver bracelet

❶ String a silver bead, a crimp bead, a silver bead, and one end of a toggle clasp on the wire. Slide the clasp and the beads to the center. Go back through the beads and the crimp with the wire. Tighten it to form a small loop around the clasp. Crimp the crimp bead (see "Basics," p. 2).

❷ Slide a bead cap and pearl onto the doubled wire. String a silver bead and a spacer on each wire (**photo a**).

**❸** On each wire, string an amethyst bead, a spacer, a pearl, and a spacer. Slide a cala link onto both wires. On each wire, string a spacer, a pearl, and a spacer (**photo b**).
**❹** Repeat step 3 three times.
**❺** On each wire, string an amethyst, a spacer, and a silver bead. Thread both wires through a pearl, a cap, a silver bead, a crimp, a silver bead, and the other clasp part. Snug up the beads, then go back through the silver beads and the crimp.
**❻** Tighten this wire to form a small loop around the clasp. Crimp the crimp bead. Cut the excess wire tails, using diagonal wire cutters.

### golden bracelet

**❶** Open a jump ring using two pliers (see "Basics"). Slide the toggle ring and the single loop on the end bar onto the jump ring. Close the ring.
**❷** Cut the beading wire in half. Pass one wire through an end bar loop. String a crimp bead and a spacer on the wire and the tail. Repeat with the second wire. String a cala link on both wires (**photo c**). Pull the wires so the tails measure 1 to 2 in. (2.5-5cm).
**❸** Crimp the crimp bead.
**❹** String a spacer, a sunstone bead, and a spacer on each long wire, then add a glass bead. String a spacer, a sunstone, and a spacer on each wire, then add a link (**photo d**).
**❺** Repeat step 4 three times.
**❻** String a spacer and a crimp on one wire. Pass the wire through a loop on the other end bar and back through the crimp, the spacer, and the link. Repeat with the other wire.
**❼** Tighten all the beads, then pull both wires to create small loops around the end

a

b

c

bar loops. Crimp the crimp. Trim the four wire tails against the two links.
**❽** Open a jump ring. Slide the toggle bar and the single loop of the endbar onto this ring. Close the ring. Open another ring. Slide the end ring and the charm on this ring. Close the ring (**photo e**).

### earrings

**❶** String a silver bead, a bead cap, an amethyst bead (**photo f**), another cap, and two more silver beads onto the head pin.
**❷** Cut the pin with diagonal wire cutters, leaving ⅜ in. (1cm) above the bead. Make a loop (**photo g** and see "Basics"). Connect an earring finding to the loop.
**❸** Make the other earring to match the first. ❂
– *Pam Arion and Julie Young*

d

e

f

g

### materials

**silver bracelet**
- **4** cala links, pewter with antique-silver finish
- **10** 6 x 9mm amethyst barrel beads
- **18** 6mm pearls
- **8** 3mm sterling silver beads
- **2** 7mm fairy skirt bead caps
- **36** 4mm heishi spacers or 3mm daisy spacers
- **2** crimp beads
- toggle clasp
- 24 in. (61cm) flexible beading wire, .014-.015

**golden bracelet**
- **5** cala links, pewter with antique-gold finish
- **4** 14 x 10mm 2-hole vintage green glass beads
- **16** 6 x 4mm sunstone beads
- **2** end bars, 2-to-1 loops, pewter with antique-gold finish
- **36** 4mm heishi spacers or 3mm daisy spacers
- **4** crimp beads
- **4** 5mm jump rings
- toggle clasp
- Art Nouveau flower charm, pewter with antique-gold finish
- 24 in. (61cm) flexible beading wire, .014-.015

**earrings**
- **2** amethyst beads
- **4** fairy skirt bead caps
- **6** 3mm silver beads
- **2** ball-end head pins
- pair earring findings

**Tools:** diagonal wire cutters, roundnose and chainnose pliers, crimping pliers

# Petal earrings

Flexible beading wire is a wonderful stringing material in many ways. Here, use it to fan out dagger beads in a flower shape to make a pair of fun earrings.

❶ Cut the wire into two 9-in.-long (23cm) lengths.

❷ String a seed bead and seven daggers on one length of wire and bring the end back through the seed bead (**photo a**).

❸ Bring both ends through the flat bead and a crimp bead. Tighten.

❹ Grasp the wires together just above the crimp with roundnose pliers and feed the ends back through the crimp to form a loop (**photo b**).

❺ Make sure the two-wire loop is small and even and there is as little slack in the wire as possible. Still holding the loop with the roundnose pliers in your nondominant hand, flatten the crimp with crimping pliers or chainnose pliers (See "Basics," p. 2 and **photo c**).

❻ Open the loop on the earring finding (see "Basics," p. 2), hang the earring, and close the loop.

❼ Make the second earring. ●
– Ellen Baird

a

b

c

## tip

### Cleaning beads

To clean and add sparkle to glass beads, put them into a container, cover with a cup or two of water, and add a tablet of denture cleaner (any brand will do). Soak them for 15 minutes, rinse, and then pat dry. – *Genie Kauhane*

**materials**

- 18 in. (46cm) flexible beading wire, .014 or thinner
- 2 flat Czech glass beads, approx. 10-12mm
- 14 10mm dagger beads
- 2 11º seed beads, matching color
- 2 silver crimp beads
- pair sterling silver earring findings

**Tools:** wire cutters, roundnose pliers, chainnose or crimping pliers

a

b

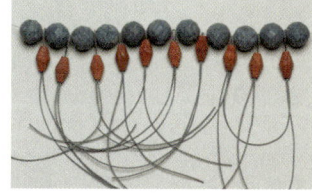

c

d

e

f

# Spangled dangles

Deck yourself out in patriotic style with this star-spangled necklace. String the base strand first, and then add the dangles.

**❶** Measure your neckline to determine the desired length of your necklace and subtract the length of your chosen clasp. Since the fringes will hang 1½-2 in. (4-5cm) below the necklace, keep the length similar to that of your neckline.

**❷** Add 6 in. (15cm) to the necklace length. Measure and cut a piece of flexible beading wire. String eleven 12mm beads to the wire's center.

**❸** Cut an 8-in. (20cm) length of cord. Fold the cord in half and position the fold over the wire between the first two 12mm beads (**photo a**). String a bicone bead over both cord ends (**photo b**).

**❹** Repeat step 3 between each pair of 12mm beads to make 10 fringes (**photo c**).

**❺** String an equal number of 12mm beads on each side of the original 11 beads until you reach the desired length.

**❻** String a crimp and one clasp half on one wire end. Pass the wire end back through the crimp and a few beads. Crimp the crimp bead (see "Basics," p. 2).

**❼** Tighten the beads and be sure the folded cords rest on the wire between the beads (**photo d**). Repeat step 6 on the other end of the wire.

**❽** Slide up each bicone bead so it is snug against the 12mm beads. Tie each set of cord ends into an overhand knot (see "Basics") under the bicone bead. Before tightening the knot, use an awl to slide the knot firmly against the bead (**photo e**).

**❾** String a star bead on each cord end so the top of the bead is ¼ to ¾ in. (6-19mm) below the bicone. Secure each star bead in place with an overhand knot (**photo f**). Stagger the distance of the stars from the bicones. Trim each cord ¼ in. below the knot and seal the ends with a dot of Fray Check. ●

– *Pam O'Connor*

## materials

- 1-2 16-in. (41cm) strands 12mm round beads
- **20** 15mm star beads
- **10** 12 x 6mm bicone beads
- flexible beading wire, .014-.019
- Conso or Stringth beading cord, size 5 or FF
- clasp
- **2** crimp beads
- Dritz Fray Check

**Tools:** crimping pliers, awl

# Stone nugget jewelry

Jewelry made with big beads in bold colors makes a strong fashion statement. One important thing to keep in mind when using big beads is that they get heavy, so you'll want to keep the length of your necklace short. Also, you'll want to counterbalance the chunky stones with a large clasp. These instructions show how to use cones to complete the three-strand design.

String each strand separately and knot between groups of beads. Tie the tails at each end together and then tie them to a wrapped loop. Thread the wire above the wrapped loop through the cone and attach the clasp with another wrapped loop. Use the leftover beads to make a matching bracelet.

## necklace

❶ Lay out the three strands of the necklace. Harmonize them by combining the accent colors used between the larger beads into the third strand. (Here, the coral in the turquoise strand and the amethyst in the citrine strand form the third strand, with coral as the dominant color.) Make the strands all the same length. These are 21 in. (53cm) long.

## materials

### necklace
- 16-in. (41cm) strand rough-faceted turquoise nuggets, 20-25mm
- 16-in. (41cm) strand faceted amethyst rondelles, 5 x 8mm
- 16-in. (41cm) strand apple coral rondelles, 6 x 10mm
- 16-in. (41cm) strand carved citrine flat ovals, 18mm
- 9 yd. (8.2m) silk or nylon bead cord, size D or 1
- 12 in. (30cm) 20-gauge gold half-hard wire
- 6-8 size 8º seed beads, any color
- 2 22mm brass cones (Ashes to Beauty Adornments, 505-899-8864)
- brass shield hook- and-eye clasp (Ashes to Beauty Adornments)
- twisted wire beading needles

### bracelet
- 12 in. flexible beading wire, .014 or .019
- gold magnetic clasp
- 2 crimp beads

**Tools:** awl, G-S Hypo Cement, wire cutters, roundnose and chainnose pliers

**Optional:** bead design board, crimping pliers

❷ You can string all the strands on flexible beading wire, but the drape that you get with cord knotted between beads is well worth the additional time. For each strand, cut a length of cord four times the length of the beads plus 12 in. (30cm). Thread a twisted wire needle to the center. String a stop bead and tie it about 6 in. (15cm) from the end of the doubled cord. Then string all the beads for the first strand. Knot between every 3-5 beads (see "Basics," p. 2).

❸ String the other two strands the same way. Then lay the three strands out flat and add beads until they are the same length.

❹ Tie the three strands together at each end with an overhand knot right against the beads (see "Basics").

❺ Cut two 5-in. (13cm) lengths of 20-gauge wire and make a wrapped loop on one end of each (see "Basics"). The loop must be large enough to prevent it from slipping through the cone's small hole.

❻ Tie one end of the necklace to a wrapped loop temporarily and pull the wire through the cone. The top of the beads should fit into the mouth of the cone so no cords or wire show. If they go too far into the cone, untie the cords and string two to three seed beads on them. Test the fit again. When you are satisfied, pass half the strands from one end through the wrapped loop in one direction and the other half through in the other direction (**figure 1**). Tie the cords to the wrapped loop with several surgeon's knots (see "Basics") and glue the knots. When dry, clip the tails to ⅛ in. (3mm). Loosely braid the three strands together and then repeat this step on the other end.

❼ Feed the wire through the cone and string a rondelle (**figure 2**)on the wire extending past the cone. Start a wrapped loop, attach the clasp, and finish the wrapped loop. Repeat on the other end.

## bracelet

❶ If you have a few leftover beads, arrange them in a pleasing pattern that is about ½ in. (1.3cm) longer than your wrist circumference.

❷ String the beads on flexible beading wire that's about 4 in. (10cm) longer than your wrist circumference.

❸ String a crimp on the end of the wire and take the wire through the loop on the clasp then back through the crimp. Crimp the crimp bead (see "Basics"). Repeat on the other end, making sure to remove almost all the slack in the bracelet. Finally, feed the wire tails through two to three beads before clipping. ◗ – *Florence Bishop*

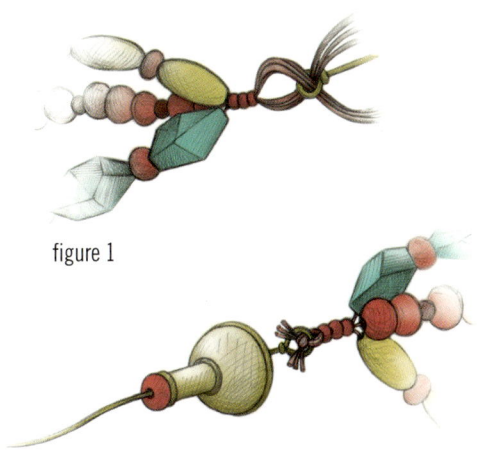

figure 1

figure 2

# Beaded hoop earrings

Unusual findings can inspire creative designs. For these earrings, dress up beaded wire hoops with four-way links and add dangles.

Ideally, you'll use 20-gauge wire for the hoop part of the earrings. But if irresistible beads just won't fit over such thick wire, use 22-gauge wire. Treat these more delicate hoops with care.

## basic earring (left and center, p. 12)

**1** For all three earrings, start with a 4½-in. (11.4cm) piece of wire. Make a loop on one end and attach it to a side loop on the link finding (see "Basics," p. 2 and **photo a**).

**2** Curve the wire into a hoop shape using a circular form like a nail polish bottle to refine the curve.

**3** For the jade earrings, make five graduated dangles with the accent beads and chain (make three for the pearl earrings): String a 2.5mm silver bead and a 6mm bead on a head pin. Start a wrapped loop above the 6mm bead (see "Basics"). Then cut five lengths of chain: two are ¼ in. (6mm), two are ½ in. (1.3cm), and one is ¾ in. (2cm) long. Attach the unwrapped loop of a dangle to the bottom link of each chain (**photo b**) and complete the wraps.

**4** String enough 4mm beads on the hoop wire to reach the bottom third of the hoop. String the end link of one of the short chains. String one 4mm bead, the medium chain, one 4mm bead, and the longest chain. This should fall at the center bottom of the hoop. If it doesn't, adjust the size of the hoop, the number of beads

between dangles, or the point at which you strung the first dangle. Repeat the pattern in reverse to string the rest of the dangles (**photo c**).

**5** String the same number of 4mm beads after the last dangle as before the first one.

**6** Shorten the hoop wire to leave ⅜ in. (1cm) for the final loop. Make the loop at a right angle to the hoop (**photo d** – it will also be at a right angle to the finding) and attach it to the finding.

**7** Make a final head pin dangle and attach it to the center loop on the finding so it hangs inside the hoop to the desired length (photo, p. 12).

**8** Attach an earring wire to the top finding loop.

## briolette earrings (right, p. 12)

Construct the earrings as above, except for the dangles.

**1** Thread a briolette on a 2½-in.- (6.3cm) long piece of 24-gauge wire or an ultra-thin head pin and position the bead about an inch (2.5cm) from one end of the wire. Bend the wire up into a circle above the stone, being careful not to chip the hole. Use chainnose pliers to bend the long part of the wire straight up at a right angle (**photo e**).

**2** Grasp the circle where the wires cross with round-nose pliers and make a single wrap around the long wire with the short end (**photo f**). Trim off the short end.

**3** If you're using an even number of chain links to hang the dangle, grasp the wire with the tip of chainnose pliers and bend it away from you perpendicular to the loop from which the briolette hangs (bend it parallel to the loop if you have an odd number of links). Begin a wrapped loop and pull the end link of the chain piece into the loop.

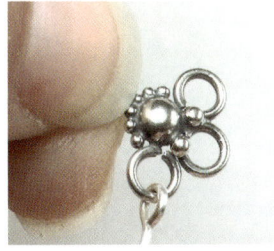

a

b

c

d

e

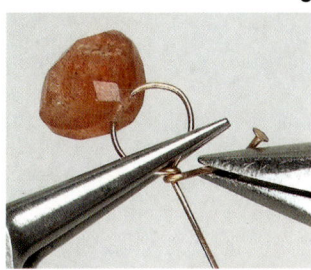

f

g

## materials

**silver and jade earrings**
- 9 in. (23cm) 20-gauge wire
- 12 2-in. (5cm) head pins
- 6 in. (15cm) silver chain
- 50 4mm Thai silver beads
- 14 2.5mm silver beads
- 12 6mm jade beads
- 2 silver 4-way connectors
- pair of earring findings

**pearl earrings**
- 9 in. 20-gauge gold-filled wire
- 6 in. gold-filled chain
- 34 4mm Swarovski crystals
- 8 gold-filled ultra-thin head pins with ball end or plain head pins and 2mm gold-filled beads
- 8 8mm oval pearls
- 42 size 11º Japanese cylinder beads
- 2 vermeil and pearl connectors
- pair of earring findings

**briolette earrings**
- 9 in. 20-gauge gold-filled wire
- 6 in. gold-filled chain
- 36 in. (.9m) 24-gauge gold-filled wire or if briolette holes are tiny, 12 26-gauge ultra-fine head pins
- 12 briolettes
- 42 4mm Swarovski bicone crystals
- 2 vermeil 6-way connectors
- pair of earring findings

**Tools:** roundnose and chainnose pliers, diagonal wire cutters
**Optional:** awl

**4** Grasp the loop at the cross with roundnose pliers and wrap the tail around the straight wire until it meets the single wrap above the briolette (**photo g**). Cut the wire off flush.

**5** If your chain is too fine to fit on the 20-gauge wire, stretch the end link with roundnose pliers or an awl. ●

*– Louise Malcolm*

# Garden charm bracelet

Combine today's playful, contemporary bead shapes to make an adorable charm bracelet—not your grandmother's charm bracelet, but a stretchy, colorful, multi-strand design with plenty of dangles to shimmer on your wrist.

**❶** To make a dangle, string a head pin with a pleasing arrangement of beads (example: a seed bead, a butterfly, and a crystal). Each dangle should vary in length from ½-¾ in. (1.3-1.9 cm), including the loop.

Make a medium-to-large-sized wrapped loop above the beads, leaving enough space for 2-3 wraps (see "Basics," p. 2). The loop should be large enough to slide over the seed beads, but smaller than the accent beads. Before completing the wrap, test the size of each loop by stringing an accent bead and a few seed beads on elastic and passing the loop over them (**photo a**).

**❷** To make dangles with beads that have a hole across the top, cut a 3-in. (7.6cm) length of wire and string the bead on the wire about ½ in. from the end. With your fingers, bend both ends of the wire up until they cross above the center of the bead (**photo b**). Use chainnose pliers to bend both wires slightly so they are parallel above the bead (**photo c**). Be careful not to crack the bead.

**❸** String an accent bead over both wires and slide it against the bend. Grasp the long wire with chainnose pliers and make a right angle about ⅛ in. (3mm) above the accent bead. Cut the short wire so it is flush with the right angle (**photo d**). Make the first half of a wrapped loop (**photo e**). Complete the wrap.

**❹** Cut five 12-in. (30cm) lengths of elastic. Tape one end of each strand and thread a twisted wire beading needle on the other end. String a mix of seed beads, dangles, and accent beads on each one. String the dangles over groups of 5 to 10 seed beads so the dangles slide. Each strand should be about ½ in. longer than your wrist circumference. As you string the strands, lay them in parallel lines to be sure the dangles are staggered along each strand (**photo f**).

**❺** String the first strand through the top hole on the spacer bar. Knot the elastic tails together with a square knot (see "Basics" and **photo g**). Keep the elastic relaxed but tight enough so it doesn't show between the beads. Dab the knot with glue, and pull it into a bead. Run the tails through a few more beads in opposite directions (**photo h**). To keep the tails in place, pull on each tail and glue the elastic where it exits the bead. After the glue is dry, trim the tail as close to the bead as possible. Repeat with the remaining strands. **❍**
– Cheryl Phelan

## materials
- Gossamer Floss or ribbon elastic
- size 11º seed beads, three colors
- assorted 2-6mm accent beads and crystals
- **30-35** assorted beads for the dangles
- spacer bar with five holes
- **30-35** 2 in. (5cm) head pins
- 9 ft. (2.7m) 22-gauge wire (makes 36 top-hole bead dangles)
- twisted wire beading needle
- G-S Hypo Cement
- cellophane or masking tape

**Tools:** roundnose and chainnose pliers, wire cutter

# tip

## Design option

Combine "angel wing" beads with a few Czech glass beads to make pretty tulip dangles. String an angel wing bead onto a head pin for the leaves. Pick up four or five seed beads or a bugle for the stem and top it with a small flower bead or pearl. Make a wrapped loop next to the top bead. – *Linda Wielgus*

# Clear bead choker

A multi-strand mix of crystals and seed beads on waxed linen makes an intriguing and irresistible necklace. Braided ends with dangles make a simple, tailored clasp.

❶ Cut six 36-in. (.9m) strands of waxed linen.

❷ String each strand with about 12 in. (30cm) of randomly placed crystals spaced with seed beads. Center the beads on the linen. As you string, lay the strands in parallel lines on your work surface and stagger the large crystals so they aren't clustered in one place. Make sure you like the way the beads are arranged and make any changes before continuing.

❸ Divide the cords on one side into three groups and braid them for 6½ in. (17cm) (photo a). This side will become the clasp's loop end.

❹ Fold the braid over into a loop so the length from beads to fold is 5 in. (13cm). Make an overhand knot (see

"Basics," p. 2). Before you tighten it, move the knot into position about 1¼ in. (3.2cm) from the fold (photo b). The knot takes up almost an inch (2.5cm) of braid, leaving about 4 in. (10cm) of braided linen on this end.

❺ Braid the cords on the other end for 4½ in. (11cm). String a large crystal onto one cord. Take another cord through the crystal in the opposite direction (it's a tight fit). Pull the two cords apart to slide the crystal toward the braid until an inch of linen extends from each side of the bead to the braid (photo c).

❻ Arrange the six cord ends so they point down toward the necklace strands. Hold all the cords together at the top of the braid and tie an overhand knot, leading with the clasp bead. Tighten the knot into place at the end of the braid and adjust the cords. After knotting, this end of the clasp should measure about 4 in. from the beaded strands to the outer edge of the clasp bead.

## materials

- spool waxed linen
- hank size 8º clear silver-lined seed beads
- **96** quartz crystal or Czech fire-polished glass beads, assorted shapes and sizes

❼ To finish the necklace, trim the tails close to the knots. For a more decorative touch, add a bead or two to each cord and secure them with an overhand knot (photo d). Vary the tail lengths slightly. ◗ – *Mindy Brooks*

# Multi-strand twist bracelet

Magnetic clasps work great on bracelets. They're strong enough to keep lightweight bracelets securely fastened, and they eliminate the frustration associated with trying to open a traditional clasp with just one hand. This easy multi-strand twist bracelet is made with strands of assorted crystals, spacers, and seed beads held together on small wrapped loops hidden inside cones. Twist it before clasping for extra flair.

❶ Cut four 21-in. (53cm) lengths of flexible beading wire. Because so many ends pass through two of the crimps, you must use the finest size, .010.

❷ Cut the silver wire into two 3-in. (7.6cm) lengths. On each wire, make a wrapped loop (see "Basics," p. 2) small enough to fit inside a cone.

❸ Center two lengths of flexible wire in each wrapped loop. Put all four ends through a crimp, sliding the crimp up to the wrapped loop (**photo a**). Crimp the crimp bead (see "Basics"). Each loop now holds four 10½-in. (27cm) lengths of wire.

❹ String a mix of seed beads, crystals, and spacers on all eight wires. Make each the length of your wrist circumference.

❺ String a crimp on the four wire ends of one group of strands. Take the ends through the loop holding the other set of strands and go back through the crimp bead. Eliminate any slack and crimp the crimp bead. Trim the excess wire. Repeat on the other side.

## materials

- **2** 12mm cones
- 7 ft. (2.1m) flexible beading wire, .010
- 6 in. 20-gauge sterling silver wire, half-hard
- **12-36** 4mm fire-polished Czech glass beads
- **12-36** 3-4mm flat sterling silver Bali spacers
- seed bead assortment, sizes 8º-12º
- **4** crimp beads
- magnetic clasp

**Tools:** roundnose and chainnose pliers, wire cutters

**Optional:** crimping pliers

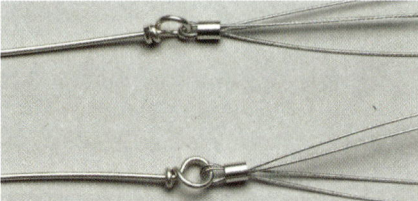

a

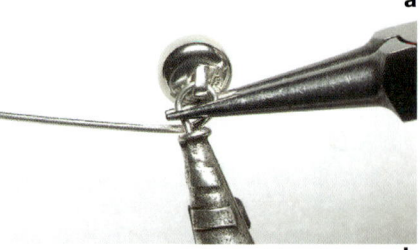

b

❻ Pass one of the silver wires through a cone from the wide end and begin a wrapped loop. Before wrapping, slip one part of the magnetic clasp onto the loop (**photo b**). Then complete the wraps. Repeat at the other end of the bracelet. ❍ – *Irina Miech*

# Multi-strand choker

A gorgeous clasp sometimes begs to be featured front and center, as does this marcasite beauty. The key to this design is attaching the strands to the clasp elegantly. Bullion wire, also called French wire, is a fine gold or silver coil used for finishing fine jewelry. A small length of coil covers the loop of cord that connects the strand to the clasp. The bullion enhances the elegant look of the clasp and also protects the cord from wear. The perfect solution!

Determine the finished length for your choker. Subtract the length of the clasp to find the strand lengths. The strands will need to vary slightly in length so they stack nicely when clasped. Before you tie the final knots, carefully try on the necklace and check the length of each strand. Tape the loose ends so the beads can't fall off. The necklace is easier to make if you work on a form. The inner strand of this necklace is 14¼ in. (36.2cm), including the clasp.

❶ Thread a needle to the center of 1½ yd. (1.4m) of Fireline. Using the cord doubled, string a pleasing combination of rondelles and seed beads. This choker has a repeating pattern of three rondelles, one seed, two rondelles, one seed, three rondelles, one seed, five rondelles, and one seed. Tape the ends of the cord before you string.

❷ Remove the tape from the ends and thread them through a ¼ in. (6mm) piece of bullion wire (**photo a**).

❸ Pass the cords through the top loop of half the clasp and back through a few beads. Position the clasp's loop in the middle of the bullion wire. Pull slowly and firmly to close the bullion loop (**photo b**).

❹ Push the beads up tight to the bullion and tie the tails between the beads with a square knot (see "Basics" p. 2 and **photo c**). Glue the knot. Take the ends through a couple more beads and tie another square knot. Repeat. Trim and glue the ends.

❺ Cut the needle from the Fireline and repeat steps 2-4 with the remaining ends and the other side of the clasp.

❻ Repeat steps 1 through 5 for the bottom strand. Test the choker before knotting off the last end of the strand. To keep the clasp straight, the bottom strand will need to be slightly longer than the top strand.

❼ Cut three 30-in. (76cm) lengths of Fireline. Thread all three strands through a ¼ in. piece of bullion (**photo d**).

❽ String a seed bead on all three cords. Pass the ends through the middle loop of the clasp and back through the seed bead. Position the clasp's loop in the middle of the bullion wire and tighten as in step 3. Tie a square knot using all six cords (**photo e**). Glue the knot.

❾ String a rondelle over all six cords and the knot (**photo f**).

❿ Thread a needle on each long strand and begin stringing seed beads, covering the short tails as you string. Knot off each short tail with a few half-hitch knots between the beads and trim the ends (**photo g**)The make a half-hitch knot, come out a bead and form a loop perpendicular to the thread between beads. Bring the needle under the thread away from the loop. Then go back over